Chosen
With Care and Love.
A GodMother offers the
strength of family, wisdom
and friendship.

DATE:

DATE:

DATE:

DATE:

DATE:

DATE:

DATE:

DATE:

DATE:

DATE:

DATE:

DATE:

DATE:

DATE:

DATE:

DATE:

DATE:

DATE:

DATE:

DATE:

DATE:

DATE:

DATE:

DATE:

DATE:

DATE:

DATE:

DATE:

DATE:

DATE:

DATE:

DATE:

DATE:

DATE:

DATE:

DATE:

DATE:

DATE:

DATE:

DATE:

DATE:

DATE:

DATE:

DATE:

DATE:

DATE:

DATE:

DATE:

DATE:

DATE:

DATE:

DATE:

DATE:

DATE:

DATE:

DATE:

DATE:

DATE:

DATE:

DATE:

DATE:

DATE:

DATE:

DATE:

DATE:

DATE:

DATE:

DATE:

DATE:

DATE:

DATE:

DATE:

DATE:

DATE:

DATE:

DATE:

DATE:

DATE:

DATE:

DATE:

DATE:

DATE:

DATE:

DATE:

DATE:

DATE:

DATE:

DATE:

DATE:

DATE:

DATE:

DATE:

DATE:

DATE:

DATE:

DATE:

DATE:

DATE:

DATE:

DATE:

DATE:

DATE:

DATE:

DATE:

DATE:

DATE:

DATE:

DATE:

DATE:

DATE:

DATE:

DATE:

DATE:

DATE:

DATE:

DATE:

DATE:

DATE:

Made in the USA
Monee, IL
11 December 2019